Winchester Cathedral Organs:
One Thousand Years

a short history

by *Andrew Parker*

INTRODUCTION

Those who are unfamiliar with the musical history of the church, and who hear the organ in regular use in today's cathedral services, may not realise that there is no official rôle for the organ in the liturgy of the church. Neither within the monastic liturgy and offices, which would have been observed *ab initio* to the Reformation, nor within the main Anglican services of Mattins and Evensong together with the Holy Communion or Eucharist is there a definite requirement for the instrument. During the age of St Swithun's Priory in Winchester (up to 1539) the daily offices of Mattins, Lauds, Prime, Terce, Sext, None, Vespers and Compline, at roughly three-hourly intervals were, along with the Mass, reliant on plainsong for the 'ordinary' (the unvarying part of the liturgical texts) and the 'propers' (those texts specfically intended for a particular saint's day or feast day within the year). After 1541, although the Latin liturgy remained, to an extent, until its final abolition in 1559, the Anglican daily Mattins (constructed out of Lauds and Prime) and Evensong (from Vespers and Compline) required new musical styles, and these, drawing on external influences towards the end of the 16th century, evolved into the 'Verse' style, consisting of sections for Solo voices alternating with Full Choir, all of which then needed accompaniment, either by the organ, or, at a slightly later stage, whilst they remained in fashion, (and if, indeed, they were ever actually used in church) with viols.

There is music notated for the organ, or for keyboard instruments in a liturgical context, in England before this date, but its function is obscure. Solo pieces for the organ, or 'Verses', exist based on plainsongs — the Winchester organist appointed following the foundation of the new Cathedral, Richard Wynslade, seems to have written two such pieces which survive in a manuscript, possibly his autograph, and one of these is based on the antiphon *Lucem tuam* which would normally have been sung with the Nunc Dimittis in Compline. Whether this sort of organ piece was to provide an alternative to the singing is not clear. The organ does seem to have had a rôle for covering processions in the Cathedral — as, for example, in 1635[1] — but its use generally would have been rather different from that today.

It must be realised that there was no habitual congregational participation in the Cathedral services until the second half of the 19th century. While, from the time of the injunctions of Bishop Horne, in 1572, it seems that there was a metrical psalm sung before the sermon on Sundays, it is not until after the Restoration, in 1660, that Winchester sources specify a rôle for the organist in the playing over of the tune. The Choir was required to sing, but the congregation was not so compelled. Possibly the organ did accompany in the years before, and this late reference comes out of a period when the authorities were anxious to define the customary practices in the musical part of the service. The 'Voluntary', which nowadays may precede the service, and covers the withdrawal of the Choir and Ministers afterwards comes from the 16th century, but again, we do not know if this was its intended function. In some other reformed churches, such music is used to cover a perio... collection is made; in the Anglican church this is often done dui

The accompaniment of the psalms for the day, which, according to the Book of Common Prayer are apportioned to the mornings and evenings of each month, is probably an 18th-century practice. The development of romantic instruments with their imitative capabilities allowed greatly for imagination in the depiction of the colourful 16th-century language of Coverdale's psalm translations. Pelicans in the wilderness, or owls in the desert, noises of the water-pipes, souls of the turtle-dove — even if some of these are probably mis-translations from the Hebrew via the Latin Vulgate — provide a rich source of inspiration for the gifted cathedral accompanist. When this first came into vogue, it was very much objected to by the tractarians'...*then came 'expressive' playing to represent sea and mountains, or thunder, or the like; it did not matter whether the voices were heard at all'.*[2] It must be remembered that these purists were striving for the reintroduction of the very plainsong psalm singing which the metrical psalms, and subsequently the chanted psalter, had displaced at least some 150 years earlier, and although they would almost have preferred entirely unaccompanied singing in church, it would probably be agreed that the organ's rôle in psalm accompaniment in the Anglican liturgy is now indispensible.

The visitor to the Cathedral will now hear an organ which is adapted to the performance of western music of all ages, both in its rôle as a solo instrument in Voluntaries and, separately, in recitals, and in its accompaniment of the Choir in the Psalms, Magnificat and Nunc Dimittis and the Anthem in a normal daily Evensong. The organ is now an essential part of the musical worship of the church.

FROM THE MIDDLE AGES TO THE REFORMATION

Whatever the uncertainties of detail concerning the organ which the 10th-century cantor, Wulfstan, described in the Old Minster in Winchester,[3] we can be reasonably sure that an instrument did exist. Despite the bizarre hyperbole of the poem, both in the description of the organ as well as details of other features of the Minster, through a careful study of the evidence in the light of other better-documented probabilities, James McKinnon[4] has concluded that the hitherto monster organ, if one were to take Wulfstan literally, can most likely be interpreted as an early mediæval instrument of about two octaves with two ranks of pipes. Built about 990, he felt that the most probable site of this instrument, which may not have had any direct liturgical function at that time, was in Ælfheah II's new works of the same period, at the eastern end of Old Minster, with part of the instrument possibly on a platform. If this is the case, and much must remain conjecture, it is quite possible that such an organ would have been able to be dismantled and transported into the completed areas of the new Cathedral when the monks carried the church's relics and other precious possessions from the neighbouring site, presumably some time after the probable consecration of the new church on April 8th, 1093, and before St Swithun's remains were moved on the feast of his Translation that year, 15th July.

While today it is easy to imagine the organ as an automatic form of accompaniment and sustaining inspiration for voices in church, we should be cautious in immediately ascribing such a rôle to the 10th-century predecessor of today's organs. That an important church such as Winchester (and that a Benedictine foundation, where great emphasis was to be placed on the rôle of music in worship) should have had an organ should not surprise us, but it has been too easy for some historians in the past to have linked the organ directly with music at this time, possibly through confusion of the word organum, which came also to describe one of the earliest forms of two-part church music.[5] The organ is often later mentioned and was used in the same way as, and together with, bells: to make a joyful noise, either to summon the people or to inform the local community of an important moment in the church's liturgy, such as the elevation of the Host at Mass. This early instrument may, then, have been more of a 'signal organ', rather than a musical instrument.

If there can be no irrefutable link between the early polyphony of the church and the organ, nevertheless, from the 12th century we certainly know of the increasing existence of organs in mediæval cathedrals. The two Winchester Tropers, coming from the end of the same period of monastic and architectural excellence in Winchester as the undertaking of the construction of the new Cathedral, show that musical art was at a contemporary zenith there. During the 12th century, when the foundation had to endure the collapse of the tower only 14 years after moving into the new building, architectural changes involving considerable work in and around the ritual choir, under the rebuilt tower, were instigated by Bishop Henry of Blois. It is reasonable to think that, in the course of all these works, something more may have been done to bring an organ into closer contact with the liturgy. This was a time when, following the rapid spread of intricate four-part polyphony from the cathedral of Notre Dame in Paris, other establishments were incorporating the new style; in the second half of the century, in Winchester itself, the scriptorium produced such supreme works as the Winchester Psalter and the great Winchester Bible. It seems most unlikely that music was not also part of this tremendous period of creative activity.

A traditional placing for mediæval organs in monastic churches was on the north side of the ritual choir, much in the same way that, because the Winchester choir is beneath the tower, the present-day organ is sited half-way along the north side, in the north transept arch. It is not an accident that in being so placed the organ should be sited above the Holy Sepulchre chapel.[6] Built as part of the new works of Henry of Blois in the middle of the 12th century, this structure, which, until it was vaulted in the early-13th century, probably had a flat wooden roof, might easily have had a dual purpose. Although the siting on the north side, or in the north transept, of a Holy Sepulchre chapel can be observed as traditional, the placing of the Winchester one between the massive pillars of the tower is unique. How much might not this structure have been an organ *pulpitum*, for which a wooden platform would have easily been strong enough to support a small mediæval instrument, and which had the happy purpose of serving also as a chapel beneath? Indeed, from the inclusion in a mention in the Winchester Cathedral Cartulary from c.1150, and again in 1172 that funds from the manor of Elindon were to be applied to *'the writing of books and the repair of the organs'*[7] we know that such an instrument must then have been in the building. When the chapel was vaulted in the 1220s,[8] at the time when the retrochoir was largely completed, and in the same contemporary style, how much might that have been not just an architectural adornment of the Holy Sepulchre chapel,[9] but a strengthening of the roof structure to take the weight of the larger sort of organ which was then being built elsewhere? Although later tradition regarded the Winchester organ's present location as being one of antiquity (and this cannot be substantiated from documentary evidence), given that the existence of an organ for the ritual choir is undisputed, it seems entirely reasonable that the instrument should have occupied its current position for a long time before we can presume that it was there at the Reformation.

While there is reference to an organ-builder in the Almoner's accounts for 1317/18,[10] the first definite mention of an organist, and therefore of the rôle of such an office and the existence of a specific organ does not come until the appointment of John Tyes in 1402.[11] By this time the musical focus had moved away from the ritual choir — the monks' choir — to the Lady Chapel, where Lady Mass and the other Marian devotions began to be adorned by polyphony which, stylistically, blossomed into one of the great musical glories of the church in England. Coming from Westminster Abbey for an initial period of twenty years, Tyes's duties included his participation in the daily singing of Lady Mass and the playing of the Lady Chapel organ. It was also planned that he should enhance the music of the monastic choir which performed polyphony on festal days, but, by implication from its clear omission, he was not to play any organ which might have been situated there, which duty must have remained with one of the monks. In 1510 Edmund Pynbrygge, who had been engaged since 1482, was contracted specifically to include playing the organs both in the Lady Chapel and in the ritual choir,[12] and it is possible that, although not mentioned in his earlier contract, there had been the same expectation of him for the previous 28 years.

THE NEW CATHEDRAL FROM 1541 TO 1850

When, following the Reformation, and the establishment of the new Cathedral Church of Winchester in 1541, the organist, Richard Wynslade, was appointed, his detailed contract[13] included the *'keaping of our organs'* as part of his daily service in the choir. Although it is not mentioned, it can be presumed that he was also to play the instrument. Owing to the lack of detail in the early Chapter Act books of the new Dean and Chapter, as well as the total loss of that Act book which would have covered the years 1600 to 1622, and the very few extant sets of any accounts between 1541 and 1642, it is not possible to give much detail about the organs in the church. If the Lady Chapel instrument survived, there is no record of it, and only after 1618 do we have any mention of organs at all in the existing accounts. In the year from November 1624 to November 1625 George Bath, the organist was paid two regular amounts of 10s for *'mending the Organs'*,[14] but this is probably just a description of the *'keeping'* defined in 1541. In 1628-29 there was a payment of 10s for *'a newe sett of keis to the Organs'*, and there are also payments for *'three pair of bellowes to the organs, & for stuffe used about them'* amounting to £1 0s 3d.[15] With what must have been a new manual, it seems that the organ in the choir received considerable attention that year. At the same time there was another 10s for *'4 newe pipes & tuning of the Rigoll'*. Since in the 17th century a regal could as much describe a small portable organ as a reed instrument, and since, clearly, it had pipes, was this a successor to the old Lady Chapel organ? The wording of Thomas Thamer's contract of 1665[16] refers to the Restoration instrument as being placed on the north side *'where the great Organ heretofore Stood'*. Was this loose wording, or was it being understood, probably by the Chapter Clerk, that the single-manual *'great Organ'* was being remembered in contrast to the *'Rigoll'*? There grew a custom, referred to in the Diary of Dean John Young,[17] of having Morning Prayer in the Lady Chapel. Perhaps this was enabled by having retained a small instrument there, but not one sufficient for the performance of organ music, for, on 18th June, 1635, at the visitation by Sir Nathaniel Brent, the Archbishop's Vicar General, they *'went in procession ways the Queer singing ane Antheme oup to our lady chapel to prayers ... and in that order we came from thence to the bodie of the churche, the organs playing a verse ...'*.[18]

In the late 18th century John Milner described the removal of the organ from over the screen to its lateral position in 1634.[19] There is absolutely no evidence to substantiate this, and it seems exceedingly doubtful that it was ever so moved; besides, with other major projects of that time, such as the vaulting of the tower, which were detailed in Dean Young's Diary, it would be extraordinary that so great an undertaking as the moving of the organ should not be discussed there. To Milner, a man of those times when so many cathedral organs had been rebuilt over a central choir screen, the position of Winchester's must have seemed very awkward and asymmetrical. Knowing that it had stood there since before the Commonwealth, Milner no doubt felt the need to explain how it had come to be there. Realising that the installation of Inigo Jones's screen, which replaced the mediæval pulpitum in 1635, would have required the demolition of anywhere a central organ could have been, he was quite content to fabricate the information that the organ had been moved from the place *'which it had occupied since the Reformation.'* Also around this time, probably on 23rd August 1635, Lieutenant Hammond, of the Norfolk Militia, visited Winchester as part of a tour of southern cathedrals. He was clearly not an expert musician, and he took much of his material at second hand, but he was only slightly impressed by the music and organs at Winchester, possibly because it was still a very simple instrument: *'The organs of this church are not exceeding faire nor rich, but sweet and tunable, and sweetly played on, by one of the rarest Organists that this Land affords, ...the Quiristers were skilfull, and the voices good, where they sing sweet and heavenly anthems'.*[20]

The organ, however, was soon to be removed — completely. In common with many other churches and cathedrals, Winchester suffered at the hands of the Roundhead troops in December 1642, and, according to Mercurius Rusticus, the Royalist pamphleteer, the organ was completely destroyed.[21] As will be seen, it was almost six years after the re-establishment of the church before a new organ could be in use, and there are signs that perhaps some of the music, *'the old bookes'* as they are referred to, may have been hidden away and have survived, although they are not extant today.[22] Could it have been that the 'Rigoll', also being portable, was similarly salted away, and could therefore have served the church until Thamer's new organ was sufficiently completed?

When the Dean and Chapter was able to take possession of the Cathedral once more, in 1660, the amount of repairs needed to the church, the Deanery and the close houses forced the building of a new organ and the refurbishment of the musical repertoire to take a relatively low priority. Perhaps there was sufficient surviving musical material to enable the choir to 'get by' during the next six years. In 1664 the small sum of £50 of the past financial year's sealing money, normally distributed to the Dean and Chapter as dividends, was set aside *'towards the charge of an Organ'*, but it was not until 1667 that greater progress seems to have been made in raising funds by selling manorial timber at Crondall.[23] Thus, although **Thomas Thamer** *'from the University of Cambridge'*[24] was contracted to build an organ on 27th July, 1665, the Chair organ to be ready before Christmas, and the Great to be completed by Michaelmas Day, 1666, either he was four years late in completing his task, or the Cathedral had to keep him waiting until November 1670 for his full payment of the £427 12s 0d which the work had cost.[25] Interestingly, this is less than the £100 which the original agreement had allowed for *'as occasion does require'*, with £400 when the Chair organ was ready, and £220 more on completion of the Great. Perhaps the delay was because the matter was in dispute, since, on 25th November 1665[26] it was ordered not to spend the money for the organ without consent, and the 1666-67 Treasurer's accounts have sums for *'Inquirendo de Thamer 2s'* and *'Literis eidem Thamero 13s 6d'*, probably both to the Dean and Chapter's legal adviser.[27]

The details of the agreement with Thamer have been printed elsewhere, on several occasions,[28] latterly with only a very few minor misreadings, and it is sufficient to summarise the contract as the specification of the 1666 organ as in Table 1.

Great	(51 notes)	Chair	(51 notes)
Open diapason	metal 8'	Principal	metal 8'
Stopped diapason	wood 8'	Stopped diapason	wood 8'
Principal	metal 4'	Flute	wood [4'?]
Recorder	wood 4'	Principal	metal 2'
Principal	metal 2'	Twenty-second	metal 1'
Principal	metal 2'		
Twelfth	metal 2 2/3'		
Fourniture	metal [II?]		
Twenty-second	metal 1'		

Table 1:   The organ by Thomas Thamer, 1666

In addition to the organ and its cases, Thamer was to build a wainscot or sounding-board behind the organ case, filling up the transept arch to the capitals.[29] This can be seen to be still in situ in the watercolour by James Cave, 1801.[30] There was subsequently an equivalent screen built on the opposite side, which must have rendered a tunnel-effect in the ritual choir. Perhaps the misunderstanding was over the construction of this second screen, for the contract specifically states that the 'faire Arch and Canopie of boards' shall 'compas over the topp of the great Organ' with no mention of the opposite side, although the amount of the reduction — almost £300 — cannot possibly represent this work alone.

One of the strangest features, and, potentially, the most difficult to understand about this organ, is its pitch. It is described as being 'Gam ut in D sol re', with the largest pipe of the Open diapason 'conteyning thirteene foot in length with his bignesse according to the Monycord'.[31] This, by reference to the monocord, seems deliberately to imply a speaking-length of 13' for bottom D, which, in relation to 16'-C for a' = 440Hz would give bottom D at 80.51Hz, or just over a quarter-tone above D sharp. This does make sense, for, when asked his recommendations about the Chair organ, possibly around 1691-92, Renatus Harris said that he proposed 'to make the pitch of the Organ halfe a noat lower and to make it Gamutt proper'.[32]

One of the greatest problems which seems to have beset the cathedral in that latter half of the 17th century was that of leaking roofs. In December 1676 repairs seem to have been required at the west end, on the south side and over the Bishop's throne,[33] and six months later, in an entry for 27th June 1677, the Chapter, with typical caution, ordered that 'the drip over ye Organ be mended, & yt it be referrd to Dr Bradshaw [the Treasurer] Mr Ken & Mr Organist yt ye Organ be mended & cleansed so farr as they judge it necessary & no further'.[34] The Treasurer's accounts for 1678-79 show Thamer to have been paid 'for mending and adding a new stopp to the Organ' a total of £41.[35] What the new stop was is not clear, but, judging from Harris's list of c.1691-2 it must have been to the Great that anything was added, and the most likely candidate would perhaps have been a mounted cornet.   Other works of comfort for the Organist included a 'fire hearth' [elsewhere a 'fire shovell'] 'for ye Organ loft' in 1674-75,[36] and a 'curtaine rod' in 1682-83,[37] but other organ repairs seem to have included '12 dayes at ye mending of ye Chayre Organ' done by one 'Jo. Joyce' for 14s in 1683-84.[38] The bellows clearly gave trouble, for Daniel Roseingrave was remunerated 10s for repairing them several times in 1685-86,[39] and Mr Coles had £1 5s 6d for the same purpose in 1689-90.[40]

At this stage the fabric of the 1666 instrument must have needed further attention, and the Dean and Chapter determined to call in the services of **Renatus Harris**. Perhaps attending

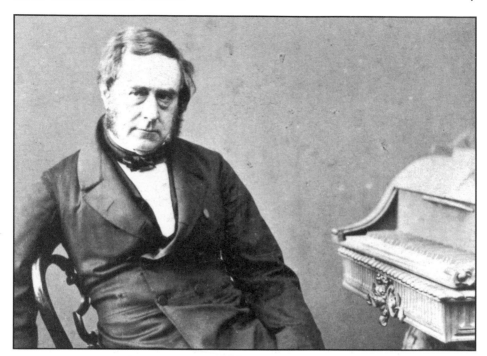

Figure 2: *Samuel Sebastian Wesley, Organist of the Cathedral from 1849 to 1865*

initially in 1691-92, when he was paid £10 *'pro opere in Organo'*,[41] his undated report on the Chair organ shows how the water damage had affected things: *'The soundboard must be taken up to be mended and cur'd of all its runnings and defects, As alsoe all the convayences. The Roller=bord I expect will serve with little alteration. But there must be a new good sett of keys.'*[42] Tonally, he also proposed revoicing the 8' Principal, Stopped diapason and 4' Flute, but of the 2' and 1' stops he said, *'The two last must be new stopps, and in place of the 22th some brisk lively double stopp, as either a furniture or double mixture'*. If this was the sequence of events, then it led, in 1693, to Harris's being asked to rebuild the Great organ as well. Whether this rebuilding re-used any materials from Thamer's instrument is not clear, and the Articles of Agreement,[43] drawn up on the 7th December 1693, for completion by 24th June 1694, included to *'make & sett up two large soundboards'* and *'three large bellowes'*, although the pipework is not necessarily specified as being 'made' or 'new'. Costing £450 the documented agreement can be interpreted in the stop list in Table 2.

If Thamer's case for the Great had originally housed eight full-compass stops and a II-rank mixture, the increase within that space to eight stops plus a II-rank and two III-rank mixtures, all of full-compass, plus a half-compass V-rank cornet must have caused some crowding, unless the two soundboards described meant that the Great was distributed about two levels. Although the Chair organ had merely been repaired, the accounts show that Harris was paid £50 *'pro novo frontispicio min: organo'* in 1693-94.[44] This was in addition to the £450, which was paid in instalments over the years 1693-94 to 1698-99.[45]

Great (50 notes)		Chair	
Open diapason	metal	[proposal for repair]	
Stopped diapason	metal	Principal	
Principal	metal	Stopped diapason	
Cornet [half compass]	metal V	Flute	
Twelfth	metal	Fifteenth [new]	
Cart	metal	Mixture	II
Fifteenth	metal		
Tierce	metal		
Larigo	metal		
Sesquialtera	metal III		
Mixture	metal II		
Furniture	metal III		

Table 2:   *The organ by Renatus Harris, 1694*

Perhaps Harris's repairs to the old warped Chair soundboard were unsuccessful. In November 1700 he was informed 'that the Organ is soe much out of Tune that the Services & Anthems cannot be play'd thereon. You are therefore desired forthwith upon receipt hereof either to come downe yor self or send a Servant to putt the said Organ in good tune according to The Articles of Agreement made between you and the said Dean & Chapter'.[46] As is indicated, Harris had contracted to attend to repair the organ whenever necessary, much as Thamer had done on receipt of his payment in 1670. While the convention of the organist being responsible for day-to-day repairs, from 1541, had still applied up to the time of the Harris partial rebuild, from thenceforth a regular payment of £8 per annum was made to the organ builder for performing what must have been regular tuning and running repairs. This sum must have covered the year-to-year maintenance, for there are no other sums in the early-18th-century accounts applying to the organ. After Renatus Harris's death his son John may have continued to receive the £8 which, since 1705, had been scheduled in the accounts as a regular outgoing, and not recorded by name. John Harris died in 1743, and the Chapter seems thereupon to have appointed **Richard Bridge**, who had probably trained in Harris's works, in his stead.[47]

If Bridge is known, according to Burney, to have died before 1776,[48] then this may have happened even earlier, for, on 25th November 1767, the Chapter ordered 'that Sir Peter Rivers Gay be empowered to employ an Organ builder to survey the Organ and make his report of it to the Chapter'.[49] Surely, from past evidence, they would have gone back to the existing organ builder, had he been alive, especially as the Dean and Chapter was paying annually for his attention? The result of this order seems to be a payment of £4 4s for 'Mr Parker the Organist's Expenses' in 1767-68.[50] Possibly Thomas Parker, of London, who built the organ for the Foundling Hospital that same year had advised the Dean and Chapter, but it is unlikely that he did any other work, for, having paid out £1 1s that year for 'Drawg Articles for Organ Builder Stamps &c'[51] and having ordered on 25th November 1768 'that the Organ be Gilt and that the Expenses thereof be paid out of the Overplus of the late Deans Leacy',[52] there were two orders for £80 to be paid to 'Mr Green the Organ Builder'.[53] From an entry in the Salisbury and Winchester Journal, discovered by Betty Matthews,[54] this was **Charles Green**, a relation of Samuel Green. He seems to have been paid a total of £188 for his work between the years 1767-68 and 1768-69, and been given £20 'together with the Old Bellows' for making new bellows that same year.[55] It is unfortunate that the articles of agreement referred to do not survive, but, from the amount paid, the work may have been confined to fairly substantial cleaning and repair, rather than new work; although a sum of 15s for *'Charcoal for the Organ Builder'* [56] perhaps shows that he was engaged in pipe-making. There must have been some construction, or reconstruction around the instrument, for John Smith, one of the Carpenters employed by the Cathedral, was paid £50 for his work on the organ in 1768-69.[57] For the following thirty years or so, the accounts and Chapter Acts are silent concerning the organ. The £8 per annum continued to be paid, and the entry in 1787-88 to *'Green for tuning organ, omitted last year'* [58] perhaps shows that Samuel Green, who had helped Charles with the Winchester College instrument before the latter's death in 1779, thereby gaining an entrée into his elder relation's work,[59] had now taken on the Cathedral tuning job. He seems not to have been very concerned to collect his money, or, perhaps, regular in his attendance, for the stipends for the years 1789 to 1791 were all paid in one lump sum in 1791![60]

This may indicate why it was not to Green, but to **John Avery**, that the Cathedral authorities turned when they next wished a major rebuild. Charles Green's work must have served sufficiently well, for, apart from 10s 6d on 25th June 1794,[61] there seem to have been no repair charges beyond the annual £8. While Avery's contract, like Green's, no longer survives, it seems that the decision was taken on 23rd June 1798[62] to seal the Agreement with Avery, who was paid £400 in two instalments: one on 1st December 1798, of £185, the remaining £215 some time during the year 1798-99.[63] The new instrument was clearly something of which the Dean and Chapter were sufficiently proud that they seem to have been able to be persuaded to make an exception to their apparent rule about holding extra-claustral musical events in the Cathedral. In the issue for 22nd July 1799 the Hampshire Chronicle could proudly report that *'The service of our Cathedral, which has been some time suspended for the purpose of erecting a new organ, is again resumed, and it is but justice to the maker (Avery) to say, that it is without doubt the first organ in the kingdom. The different stops are beautifully aided by the pedals, which are twelve in number, and played by the feet.'* [64] On the mornings of the 19th and 20th September, the Hampshire Music Meeting was allowed to hold two performances in the Cathedral, the first of Handel: *Messiah*, the second a 'Grand Selection' from the sacred works of Handel. *'In the course of each mornings performance Mr Chard* [the festival's director, and the *de facto* assistant to the aged Peter Fussell, the Cathedral organist] *will play a Concerto on the New Organ built by Avery, in order to shew the different stops.'* [65] According to Hamilton's Catechism, Avery *'retained, of the old organ, only the front pipes and some of the movement'.*[66]

In the early 19th century Henry Leffler [67] noted the specification of this organ, which is listed in Table 3.

Although, since the article in the Christian Remembrancer of 1834,[68] much has been made of Avery's later dissolute habits, and his tendency of 'borrowing' pipes from one organ to finish another, which was then left incomplete, Winchester seems to have fared better in his hands. His instruments were, apparently, known for their combination of *'quantity with quality in every department; the compound stops being very brilliant and sprightly, and the reeds rich and quick in their speech...'* [69] There is nothing in the way of unusually large or extraordinary payments to craftsmen to show whether Avery's work involved major alterations to Thamer's main case, but, judging from Cave's painting about two years after the rebuild,[70] it would seem unlikely that it was capable of any convenient extension at the sides. Although it seems to stand well within the transept arch, its height and depth were governed by the Chair case in front and the sounding-board behind. Indeed, this must have been one of the major limitations, and

Great		Swell		Choir	
57 notes: GG - e'''		34 notes: g - e'''		57 notes: GG - e'''	
Great open diapason		Open diapason		Dulciana (from c)	
Open diapason		Stopped diapason		Stopped diapason	
Stopped diapason		Principal		Principal	
Principal		Cornet	III	Flute	
Twelfth		Trumpet		Fifteenth	
Fifteenth		Hautboy			
Sesquialtera	III				
Mixture	II				
Cornet (from c)	IV				
Trumpet					

Table 3:   *The organ by John Avery, 1799*

provides perhaps the major reason for the plan to abandon an otherwise fine case in 1824. Avery's Swell is typical of its period, and the short compass would have enabled it to fit in a reasonably compact box, but there can have been no room left in the case for any future expansion, if, indeed, such a thing was ever contemplated at that time.

In a climate of increased interest in the restoration of the cathedral fabric, perhaps encouraged by John Milner's *History and Survey of the Antiquities of Winchester*, there was considerable discussion and much dissention over plans to replace the 17th-century choir screen and rearrange the choir seating.[71] While the first stage of this work was undertaken with common enthusiasm, and the Inigo Jones screen was removed in 1819 to make way for a gothic design of William Garbett's, the further part of the plan, to remove the organ and place it over the screen, only reached the stage of the removal of the instrument from the north transept arch. It was intended to place galleries in the openings created by removing the sounding-boards in both crossing arches, and, in an age when the ritual choir of a cathedral had often been an exclusively male preserve,[72] this might enable a female viewpoint for the services. Hence, the gallery which remains on the south side of the choir became known as the 'Ladies' Gallery'.

With uncertainty over a final decision on the organ, and with the Thamer case presumably destroyed, the remainder of the works were stored, for a number of years as it turned out, in the north transept, which only a few years before had been cleared out of detritus which had rendered it like a *'common work-shop'*.[73] In June 1822 the Dean tried, without much success, to get the 1819 decision reversed, and, with equality of votes for and against, nothing was done.[74] The report of the Organist, George Chard, and then that, more particularly, by the Vice-Dean and Canon Iremonger, who insisted that the wording be recorded in the Chapter Book at the June Chapter in 1823, that *'the Organ has suffered already materially by the posture in which the pipes are laid and the Damp of the Floor and another Winter will of course increase the injury and require a consideration of the best Mode of preserving it'*[75] finally brought in the expertise of **Benjamin Blyth** the following month. Eventually, the Dean having himself given £100 towards the cost of replacing the organ in *'its ancient position'*, the 1819 vote was rescinded and Blyth was engaged to rebuild the organ.[76] Whether or not Thamer's case had already been destroyed, the sounding-boards behind had been removed, and, the case having been so crowded before, it was in the spirit of the time to engage Edward Blore to design one which sought, perhaps too rigidly, to blend with the 14th-century choir stall canopies.[77] While this case was viewed with scorn by Wesley ('*a sorry affair*')[78] and even this century has been defiled as 'mock-Gothic match-boarding',[79] Blore was an antiquarian who had trained in that field as a draughtsman, and his case, which is the one seen today, is not really the poor exercise for which it has been derided; and especially not when one considers the interminable indecision which may well have seen its predecessor deteriorate beyond repair. In any event, Blore's case entirely filled the arch laterally, and thus provided more space for the rebuild.

Once again, history has not allowed us to view the details of Blyth's contract: we can observe the Chapter decision '*to proceed in the construction and erection of the organ with the general swell*' in 1823,[80] and we can see that he was paid £490 15s 6d in 1824-25 for his work.[81] It is, however, possible to extrapolate that this rebuild used the majority of Avery's work. One thing which changed, since Thamer's Chair organ case (with Harris's new front) had also been removed, was the position of the Choir case to a lower level beneath the feet of the organist and within the actual structure of the choir stall canopies. This allowed the front of Blore's case to come much further forward than its predecessor. Described as '*the preposterous organ case, with its contemptible box of reeds below*',[82] it seems that the upper parts of three of the stalls beneath were appropriated to house a department which must have shouted into the ears of the Cantoris side congregation.[83] The following year, horizontal bellows were installed, the others '*being irreparable and horizontal Bellows being generally used*'.[84] While Blyth was to have had £80 for this '*as per Contract*', the entry is struck through in the accounts,[85] so, presumably, it was determined that he had already been paid for this eventuality. It was not until 1838 that Blyth was employed to install a double diapason for the pedal, instead of the pull-downs which he must have re-installed from Avery's design, but to which he seems to have provided a partial octave of unison pipes. '*The present Pedal Keys from the different arrangement being entirely useless two Octaves of German Pedal Keys [were] to be added with movement to act either separately or together on the Great Organ and Choir Organ Keys as well as the Pedal Pipes alone, also a Draw-Stop to shut off the Pedal Pipes when required.*'[86] Although contracted to do this work for £154, with some extra work Blyth was paid a total of £202 10s during 1837-38.[87]

In November 1845 £150 was ordered '*for improving the organ*'[88] which seems to have resulted in **James Blyth**, Benjamin's son, extending the short Swell by one octave downwards, and his moving of the blowing apparatus and bellows, including a cranked rotary action, to the Holy Sepulchre chapel beneath.[89] The specification of the organ at this stage is listed in Table 4.[90]

One remaining question concerning the organs before the 1850s is that of regular access to the instrument. Once the choir stalls were installed, after 1308, there can have been no direct way up from the ritual choir, if that had ever been intended, and, although perhaps a simple ladder-arrangement may have sufficed, another system must, surely, have been adopted. For an access from outside the choir, the most natural course would have been to have some form of narrow staircase in the eastern part of the north nave aisle, rising in the bay to the west of the tower, and adjoining the western end of the platform above the Holy Sepulchre chapel, thus leaving access to the chapel itself clear. After 1666, a straightforward door in the wainscot behind the case would have allowed the organist to pass through the gap between the western side of the case and the tower pillar to the choir side of the instrument. Somers Clarke[91] tells us of an access via a stair inside Garbett's screen, and so, presumably, along the top of the stalls on the North side. Although there are no surviving architectural drawings, a stair inside such a structure, and, also, inside its 17th-century predecessor, would have been very likely, and perhaps this formed the main route to the organ. The mediæval pulpitum

Great
1 Open diapason -- metal
2 Open diapason -- wood
3 Stopped diapason
4 Principal
5 Twelfth
6 Fifteenth
7 Tierce
8 Sesquialtera
9 Mixture
10 Trumpet

Choir
1 Stopped diapason
2 Dulciana
3 Flute
4 Principal
5 Fifteenth
6 Clarabella
7 Cremona

Swell
1 Stopped diapason
2 Open diapason
3 Principal
4 Cornet
5 Trumpet
6 Hautboy

Pedal
1 Unison open diapason --
   wood
2 Double diapason -- wood

Couplers
Choir and swell to great
Choir to great
Pedal to great
Pedal to choir

Table 4:   *The organ by Benjamin and James Blyth, c.1846*

would also have had some sort of stair, and it may be that the way along the tops of the stalls was an ancient one.

In 1846 the blowing plant seems to have moved down into the Holy Sepulchre chapel, as has been mentioned. This is probably the stage at which a hole was first made in the vault of the western chapel—a kind of vandalism which was not atypical of its age! Although, at first, this would have freed up space in the case, the puzzle is the single reference in the Chapter Acts of 1850, *'that the Stair Case leading up to the Organ be restored to its Old Position'*.[92] This is before the Willis organ had been thought of—possibly even by its maker—and can have nothing to do with that. It has been suggested that this was to make a personal staircase for Wesley, with chit-chat tradition connecting it with his penchant for fishing;[93] but this must be sheer non-sense. No Dean and Chapter would have acted for any such reasons. If the *'Old Position'* was the access from the aisle and transept side of the platform, then perhaps the iron spiral staircase installed in the Holy Sepulchre chapel was equivalent to access from outside the choir, rather than the more public route along the tops of the stalls, and so could be called the *'Old Position'*.

THE ORGAN FROM WILLIS TO HARRISON

The history of the organ seen in the Cathedral today begins with the Great Industrial Exhibition of 1851. While gradual improvements had been made under Benjamin and James Blyth, who had died in 1840 and 1847 respectively, the instrument was, most probably, in an un-happy state. It had been conceived as a late-18th-century organ with rather ad hoc additions, and did not accord with the principles of the much better instruments then being con-structed. Soon after Samuel Sebastian Wesley arrived in Winchester, following George Chard's death in 1849, the three-manual organ exhibited by the young Henry Willis in London, among the other thirteen instruments in the Great Exhibition, must have seemed to provide an ideal opportunity for a ready-made improvement to the situation in the Cathedral.[94] Although the London scheme needed considerable rearrangement to fit within the limited space of Blore's 1824 case, so that the 70-stop 3-manual organ became a 48-stop 4-manual instrument, the cost was an astronomical £2,500. Of this, the Dean and Chapter contributed £500, but the remainder had to be raised by public subscription, for the first time in Winchester.[95] There is no surviving account of this fund, which, from notices in the press,[96] was to have provided for restoration work to the altar screen in addition to the organ, but it seems that the donations to the fund fell well short of expectation,[97] competing, as it was, with the Patriotic Fund for the Crimean War, but, presumably, the money must have been achieved somehow. There is no doubt that Wesley's personal interest in this matter deflected any of his other passions, particularly that of fishing. From the register,[98] it is possible to observe that while his dedication to duty at services could normally be somewhat spasmodic, during the time that the organ was actually being installed by Willis, from the beginning of 1854, Wesley was in attendance daily! There was, apparently, some worry about the weight of the organ to be borne by the Holy Sepulchre chapel structure, which delayed its opening, and, when it was first heard in public, on 3rd June 1854, *'the pedal and choir organs, and the grand organ trumpets and clarions were silent'*.[99] Nevertheless, a choir of about 50 with *'vocal celebrities'* from many other cathedrals and a congregation of about 1500 attended.[100] The official opening recital on the completed instrument was given on 28th November 1854 by Wesley.[101]

Lack of space precludes the listing of Willis's original 1851 specification here.[102] Wesley, as Nicholas Thistlethwaite has remarked, *'was able to make some economies by eliminating most of the duplication in the specification, but he then chose to retain complete choruses in each division (apart from the solo, which was anyway an addition) at the cost of strings, flutes and imitative reeds.'*[103] Willis had the foresight to prepare the soundboards of the Swell for one or two stops on light pressure wind, and the Solo similarly. The apparent confining of the Barker-lever action to the Great and Swell must imply that the Choir, Solo and Pedal divisions had entirely tracker action.[104] There are no surviving drawings showing the disposition of the organ within the case, but, from statements as to what was altered at a later date, it would seem most likely that the Choir was at the front, at impost-level, with the Great above, the Swell behind, and the Solo perhaps over the Swell. The Pedal must have been distributed at the sides.

The history and development of the 1854 organ has depended, on the one hand, upon necessary renewals and updates of the mechanical fabric, while, on the other, and to a major degree, it has hinged on solutions to the problem of enabling the instrument to support congregational singing in the Nave. In 1854 this was no problem at all. It is only from the start of the meetings of the Church Choral Association for the County of Hampshire, held triennially from 1866,[105] after Wesley had left Winchester, that there were occasions when the Nave would have been used on a large scale. The replacement of Garbett's gothic screen with Scott's happy re-working of the design of the 14th-century return stalls, as an open-work, slim divide between nave and ritual choir, in 1871 would have allowed a nave congregation to have both the view into the choir, and to feel nearer to the source of the music; but this was no solution to musical support for several hundred voices.

The rebuild by Willis in 1898 saw a major redistribution of the divisions within the case. The installation throughout of tubular pneumatic action allowed the soundboards to be placed in different, relatively unmechanically related, positions. The blowing plant had been augmented with a hydraulic engine in 1887, but new bellows had been installed in 1888-9 and

Pedal		**Double trumpet**	16'	**Solo (enclosed)**	
Double open diapason	32'	Trumpet	8'	Viola di gamba	8'
Open diapason	16'	Clarion	4'	Vox angelica	8'
Violone	16'			Concert flute	4'
Bourdon	W 16'	**Swell (enclosed)**		Piccolo	2'
Octave	8'	Double diapason	16'	Cor anglais	8'
Superoctave	4'	Open diapason	8'	Clarinet	8'
Mixture	III	Violin diapason	H 8'	**Solo (unenclosed)**	
Grand bombard	H 32'	Lieblich gedacht	8'	Tuba	8'
Bombard	H 16'	Lieblich flöte	4'	Tuba clarion	4'
Ophicleide	16'	Principal	4'		
Clarion	8'	Twelfth	2 2/3'	**Couplers**	
		Fifteenth	2'	**(tubular pneumatic)**	
Great		Mixture	III	Swell to great	
Double open diap. No.1	H 16'	Contra posaune	16'	Choir to great	
Double open diap. No.2	16'	Cornopean	8'	Solo to great	
Open diapason No.1	H 8'	Hautboy	8'	Swell to choir	
Open diapason No.2	H 8'	Vox humana	8'	**(mechanical)**	
Open diapason No.3	8'	Clarion	4'	Swell to pedal	
Open diapason No.4	8'	Tremulant		Great to pedal	
Doppel flöte	H 8'			Choir to pedal	
Claribel flute	8'	**Choir (unenclosed)**		Solo to pedal	
Principal No.1	H 4'	Open diapason	8'		
Principal No.2	4'	Claribel flute	8'		
Principal No.3	4'	Gamba	8'		
Flauto traverso	H 4'	Dulciana	8'		
Flûte harmonique	4'	Flute	4'		
Twelfth	2 2/3'	Piccolo	2'		
Fifteenth	2'	Orchestral oboe	8'		
Mixture	III	Corno di bassetto	8'		

Table 6:   *The organ, 1905, showing additions by Hele (H), and by Willis in 1898 (W)*

The major work was undertaken by Harrisons in 1937-1938, when what had been a Willis organ with Hele accretions was turned into an instrument which was voiced, in the famous Harrison style, to blend well throughout. Electro-pneumatic action was the godsend. This enabled the console to be detached, for the first time, and so the entire Blore case was freed for the pipes and action. With the console's move to the south side of the nave twelfth bay at organ-case floor-level, the spiral stair, which for so long had mutilated the Holy Sepulchre chapel, could be removed. This moving of the console also allowed for a new design, which, although it did not go as far as the proposals which had been raised in 1922, splitting the organ into north and south choir cases, did move the Choir division into the twelfth bay of the north nave. In any case, Hele's bombards had occupied the site behind this arch at north-aisle floor-level since 1905, there being absolutely no room anywhere else for additional pedal pipes, and space, always at a premium in the Winchester designs, meant that there had to be a certain amount of 'borrowing', particularly (and not at all unusually) in the Pedal department. Overall, the effect was to create a late-romantic English instrument of much distinction.

Pedal

1	Double open wood (from 2)	32'
2	Open wood	16'
3	Open diapason	16'
4	Violone (from 25)	16'
5	Bourdon	16'
6	Dulciana (from 17)	16'
7	Octave wood (from 2)	8'
8	Principal (from 3)	8'
9	Flute (from 5)	8'
10	Fifteenth (from 8)	4'
11	Mixture 17 19 22	III
12	Bassoon (from 54)	16'
13	Contra bombard (from 14)	32'
14	Bombard	16'
15	Ophicleide	16'
16	Posaune (from 15)	8'
	Choir to pedal	
	Great to pedal	
	Swell to pedal	
	Solo to pedal	

Choir (unenclosed)

17	Contra dulciana	16'
18	Open diapason	8'
19	Claribel flute	8'
20	Gamba	8'
21	Dulciana	8'
22	Gemshorn	4'
23	Flute	4'
24	Piccolo	2'
	Swell to choir	
	Solo to choir	

Great

25	Double open diapason	16'
26	Open diapason No1	8'
27	Open diapason No2	8'
28	Open diapason No3	8'
29	Open diapason No4	8'
30	Doppel flute	8'
31	Claribel flute	8'
32	Principal No1	4'
33	Principal No2	4'
34	Principal No3	4'
35	Harmonic flute	4'
36	Flauto traverso	4'
37	Octave quint	2 2/3'
38	Superoctave	2'
39	Mixture 12 15 17 19 22	V

40	Double trumpet	16'
41	Trumpet (harm tr)	8'
42	Clarion (harm tr)	4'
	Choir to great	
	Swell to great	
	Solo to great	

Swell (enclosed)

43	Double diapason	16'
44	Open diapason	8'
45	Violin diapason	8'
46	Lieblich gedackt	8'
47	Echo salicional	8'
48	Vox angelica (from c)	8'
49	Principal	4'
50	Lieblich flute	4'
51	Twelfth	2 2/3'
52	Fifteenth	2'
53	Mixture 17 19 22	III
54	Contra oboe	16'
55	Oboe	8'
	Tremulant	
56	Contra posaune	16'
57	Cornopean (harm tr)	8'
58	Clarion (harm tr)	4'
	Octave	
	Suboctave	
	Solo to swell	

Solo (enclosed)

59	Viola da gamba	8'
60	Voix celeste (from c)	8'
61	Harmonic flute	8'
62	Concert flute	4'
63	Harmonic piccolo	2'
64	Clarinet	8'
65	Orchestral oboe	8'
66	Tromba	8'
	Tremulant	

Solo (unenclosed)

67	Tuba (harm)	8'
	Octave	
	Suboctave	
	Unison off	

Table 7:   *The organ by Harrison and Harrison, 1938*

1   See below, p.4

2   The Ecclesiologist No.XXV, September 1843, p.3

3   The description is a metrical prologue to a history of the life of S. Swithun. See CAMPBELL, Alistair, ed.: *Frithegodi Monachi Breviloquium Vitae Beati Wilfredi et Wulfstani Cantoris Narratio Metrica de Sancto Swithuno*, Zurich, 1950.

4   McKINNON, James W.: The tenth-century organ at Winchester in *The Organ Yearbook*, Vol.V (1974), p.4 ff

5   See the entry for Organ in *The New Grove*, *passim* and particularly section IV,6 The church organ 1100-1450 on the dangers of conjection from musical iconography.

6   See PARK, David: The wall paintings of the Holy Sepulchre chapel in *British Archaeological Association Conference Transactions* for 1980 (Winchester Meeting), published 1983, pp.38-62 for a detailed discussion of the dating of aspects of the chapel structure.

7   WCA, Winchester Cathedral Cartulary, vol.1 second foliation, ff.2v,(1107 and c.1150) and 1v (1172) in GOODMAN, A.W., ed.: *The Chartulary of Winchester Cathedral*, Winchester, 1927, 5, 10, 3

8   Park, *op. cit.* p.48 and fn 87, 88

9   It is now thought that the remodelling was linked to Peter des Roches, Bishop of Winchester (1205-1238), one of the leaders of the crusades, who took the cross in 1221. See PARK, David and WELFORD, Peter: The medieval polychromy of Winchester Cathedral in CROOK, John ed.: *Winchester Cathedral — Nine Hundred Years*, Chichester, 1993, pp.123-138 at p.128

10   WCA Account of Almoner, 1317-1318 in KITCHIN, *Compotus Rolls*, 404

11   WCA Registers of Common Seal [RCS] Vol.I (1345-1497), f.15v

12   For Pynbrygge's contracts see WCA RCS Vol.I, f.106v (1482) and *ibid*. Vol.II, f.44v (1510). A detailed discussion of the musical implications of the contracts and the functions of the organists can be found in BOWERS, Roger: The Lady Chapel and its Musicians c1210 - 1559 in CROOK, *op. cit.*, pp.249-258 at p.252 f

13   WCA RCS Vol.IV, f.15r

14   WCA Treasurer's Accounts [TA] 1624-1625, *Varia*, p.21 two entries dated 18 Dec 1624 and 20 Jun 1625 currently under call number T4/3/7/4

15   WCA TA 1628-1629, *Varia*, p.17, 19 Aug 1629

16   WCA Organ Miscellany [Org Misc] — papers relating to the organ.

17   WCA Covering the years 1618 - 1642, extracts were published in GOODMAN, Frances ed.: *Tne Diary of Dean John Young*, Winchester, 1923

18   *Ibid*. in the original MS, p.88

19   MILNER, John: *The History ... and Survey of the Antiquities of Winchester*, 2 vols. Winchester 1798-, Vol.2, p.37. Milner's comments on p.33 are about the general purposes of mediæval pulpita, rather than saying that the Winchester one was specifically used in any particular manner, for which no evidence exists.

20   [HAMMOND], Lieutenant: A relation of a short survey of the western counties... in *Royal Historical Society Camden Miscellany* 16, Camden 3rd Ser., 52

21   Mercurius Rusticus *(pseud.)* [Bruno RYVES] XX week, p.161, dated 24 Feb 1643/4

22   For further on this topic see PARKER, Andrew: The Cathedral Choir and its Music, 1660 - 1800 in CROOK, *op. cit.*, pp.305-314, at p.305 ff

23   WCA CA 1660-1695 p.98 (dated 1 Dec 1664) and p.141 (dated [9] Dec 1667).

24   See reference to Thamer's contract, note 16 above and note 31 below

25   WCA Chapter Orders [CO] p.25 dated 21 Nov 1670

26   WCA CA 1660-1695, p.114 dated 25 Nov 1665

27   WCA TA 1666-1667, *Varia*

28   See PIPER, A. Cecil: Notes on Winchester Cathedral Organs in *The Organ*, Vol.I (1921-1922) p.177 f; WILLOUGHBY, G. St M.: The Organs of Winchester Cathedral in *The Organ*, Vol.IX (1929-1930) p.2 f; and, more accurately in MATTHEWS, Betty: *The Organs and Organists of Winchester Cathedral*, 3rd Edition, Winchester 1975, p.5 f

29   *ibid*.

30   Winchester Cathedral Triforium Gallery Acc.No. 1143

31   See Thamer's contract *passim*

32   WCA Org Misc

33   WCA CO p.44 dated 7 Dec 1676

34   *ibid*. p.45 dated 27 Jun 1677

35   WCA TA 1678-1679, *Varia*, three separate entries

36   WCA TA 1674-1675, *Varia*, 3 Mar 1674/5, 1s 6d

37   WCA TA 1682-1683, *Varia*, "Mending lockes and keyes & curtaine rod in ye Organ loft & other work by Eeton 11s 4d"

38   *ibid*.

39   WCA TA 1685-1686, *Varia*, dated 25 Jan 1685/6

40   WCA TA 1689-1690, Summary of Accounts, p.12

41   WCA Treasurer's Accounts in Book [TB] 1691-1692, f.18 *Varia*, "Mro Harris pro ope in Organo £10 0s 0d" also "Pro instrumento musico in schola choristarum £3 10s 0d"

42   WCA Org Misc Harris report

43   WCA Org Misc

44   WCA TB 1693-1694 f.52, *Varia*

45   WCA TB 1693-1694 f.52, *Varia*, "Mro Harris per condendo novo organo £100 0s 0d"; *ibid*. 1694-1695 f.59 "Mro Harris Organorum Fabro £70"; *ibid*. 1695-1696 f.72 "Solut Mro Harris Organorum Fabro £70"; *ibid*. 1696-1697 f.84v "Dno Harris Organorum Fabro £70"; *ibid*. 1697-1698 f.95v "Mro Harris Organorum Fabro £70"; *ibid*. 1698-1699 f.106 "Mro Harris Organorum Fabro per anno 1699 et ultim. portion. £70"

46   WCA Org Misc, draft letter dated 25 Nov 1700

47   WCA CA 25 Nov 1743, but see also the "Foul Chapter Book" (i.e. the rough book) 1739-1770 f.13, 25 Nov 1743 "Ordered that Edwd Bridge [Mr Bray - erased] do succeed Mr Harris in his care of ye Organ with the same Salary"

48 HOPKINS, Edward and RIMBAULT, Edward: *The Organ*, 3rd ed., London 1877, p.144 "We learn ... from a note in Burney's History, that [Bridge] died before 1776." This note has not been traced.
49 WCA CA 1739-1776 p.325, dated 25 Nov 1767
50 WCA TB 1752-1776 p.237
51 *ibid.*
52 WCA CA 1739-1776 p.334, dated 25 Nov 1768
53 WCA CA *loc. cit.* and p.339, dated 23 Jun 1769
54 See MATTHEWS, *op. cit.* p.9 and MATTHEWS, Betty: Samuel Green and his relations in *The Organ*, Vol.LVI (1977) p.19 ff
55 WCA CA 1739-1776 p.346, dated 25 Nov 1769
56 WCA TB 1752-1776 p.251, 1768-1769, *Varia*
57 *ibid.* p.248, 1768-1769, Repairs of the Church
58 WCA TB 1777-1793 p.219, 1787-1788
59 See MATTHEWS, Samuel Green... *op. cit.*
60 WCA TB 1777-1793 p.291, [Stipends]
61 WCA TB 1793-1807 p.[8], 1793-1794
62 WCA CA 1776-1803 p.325, "That the Chapter seal be set to an Agreement with Mr John Avery for rebuilding the Cathedral Organ"
63 WCA TB 1793-1807 p.111, 1797-1798 1 Dec 1797 "Avery in part, as per Agreement for rebuilding the Organ £185" and *ibid.* p.[67] 1798-1799 "Mr Avery in full for the Organ £215"
64 *Hampshire Chronicle* [HC] of 22 Jul 1799 p.4c
65 HC of 16 Sep 1799 p.4e
66 See HAMILTON, J.A.: *Hamilton's Catechism of the Organ*, 4th edition, London, 1865, p.86
67 See PEARCE, Charles William: *Notes on English Organs of the period 1800-1810 ... from the manuscript of Henry Leffler*, London [1912], p.75
68 See Organo-Historica No. XIV in *Christian Remembrancer*, 1834, p.375
69 *ibid.*
70 See note 30 above
71 The most recent account of this period of restoration and change is BARRETT, Philip: Georgian and Victorian restorations and repairs, 1775-1900 in CROOK, *op. cit.*, pp.313-328
72 See On the arrangement of our Cathedrals in *The Ecclesiologist* No.XVI, November 1842, pp.[33]-35
73 WCA CA 1804-1824 p.278, dated 25 Nov 1816
74 WCA CA 1804-1824 p.424, dated 25 Nov 1822
75 WCA CA 1804-1824 p.430, dated 21 Jun 1823
76 WCA CA 1804-1824 p.450, dated 10 Apr 1824
77 See comments on this *passim* in THISTLETHWAITE, Nicholas: *The making of the Victorian organ*, Cambridge 1990, p.82
78 See A letter of S.S. Wesley in *Musical News*, Vol.XXVII (1904), p.426
79 RHODES, Harold: The Music of the Cathedral in *Winchester Cathedral Record* XVIII (1948), pp.15-18
80 WCA CA 1804-1824 p.441, dated 25 Nov 1823
81 WCA TB 1823-1837 p.80, 1824-1825, Repairs to the Church
82 Anonymous letter dated Winchester, 9 Jul 1825, in HC for 11 Jul 1825, p.2d
83 See CLARKE, Somers letter dated 3 Sep 1922 in *The Organ*, Vol.II (1922-23), p.123-5
84 WCA CA 1824-1850 p.40, dated 19 Nov 1826
85 WCA TB 1823-1837 p.169, 1826-1827 Repairs to the Church
86 WCA Org Misc, Agreement with Blyth dated 19 Feb 1838
87 WCA TB 1838-1845 p.16, 1837-1838 Various "Alteration of the Organ £202 10s"
88 WCA CA 1824-1850 p.368, dated 25 Nov 1845
89 CLARKE, *op. cit.* p.123. He says he first saw the organ in 1848, (when he would have been aged but 7).
90 See HAMILTON, *op. cit.* pp.86-87 (also editions for c.1838 and 1842 and 1855, although not all with specifications)
91 CLARKE, *op. cit.* p.123
92 WCA CA 1824-1850 p.442, dated 26 Mar 1850
93 See MATTHEWS, Betty: The Organs... *op. cit.* p.26 "When the new organ was installed he persuaded those in charge to build him a private stairway and this was done...". See also RANNIE, J.A.: The rebuilt organ at Winchester Cathedral in *The Organ*, Vol.XVIII (1938-1939) p.204 and CLARKE, *op. cit.* (note 82 above)
94 There is no sign of Wesley's often-discussed persuasion of the Dean and Chapter to buy a modified form of Willis's instrument in the Chapter records, but it is clear that some additional advice was being sought when, on 25th Nov 1853, the Chapter ordered "That the defects in the organ render it inexpedient to spend any large sum of money on its renewal; and the experts are of the opinion that a new organ should be purchased".
95 The £500 was given by order of Chapter (WCA CA 1850-1876 p.52) on 26 Nov 1853. It is clear that they had not, even by then, definitely settled on the purchase of the Willis organ, for the money was voted "...for the improvement of the present organ, or if it be thought more adviseable, towards the purchase of a New Organ for the Cathedral." In a letter to the *Hampshire Chronicle*, dated 1 Dec 1853 (HC 3 Dec 1853 p.8e), the Dean stated that the new organ was to cost £2,500. Willis allowed £400 for the old organ, which was moved to Christ Church, Lancaster Gate, in London.
96 HC 11 Mar 1854 p.4a for first notice of the increased scope of the fund.
97 HC 27 May 1854 p.4a "...instead of having a surplus in hand, the sum received and promised is not such as to justify [the Dean] in holding out any hopes of the Restoration of the Altar Screen."
98 WCA Attendance Register 1852-1864, entries 10 Jan 1854 onwards.
99 HC 10 Jun 1854 p.4c
100 *ibid.* Cathedrals contributing "vocal celebrities" included Durham, St Pauls, Westminster Abbey, Ely, Chichester and Salisbury.
101 HC 2 Dec 1854 p.4d The remainder of the organ not used in the Winchester re-design went to America, according to RHODES: The...Organ (see note 117 below)
102 See POLE, William: *Musical Instruments in the Great Industrial Exhibition of 1851*, London 1851, pp.68-72

103 THISTLETHWAITE, *op. cit.* p.417
104 WCA CA 1850-1876 pp.73-75 Specification and additional information as provided to Dean and Chapter by Willis. See also POLE *op. cit.* p.70 concerning Barker-lever action used in the 1851 version of the instrument.
105 See, for example, reviews in HC *passim*, and, further afield, in the *Musical Standard*, 1866, 1869, 1872, 1875, etc.
106 A gas engine was considered in 1887, but water-power was installed instead (WCA CA 1876-1896 pp.251, 254, 256, Jan - May 1887). New bellows are mentioned on 23 Jun 1888 (*ibid.* p.280) and a fund for them on 25 Nov 1889 (*ibid.* p.305), and this must be the date of the move to the triforium.
107 WCR Vol.VI (1937), p.5 concerning the repair of the organ: "...its reconstruction will enable us to do away with the ugly excrescence which now protrudes into the north transept."
108 Full specification and additional information was given in HC 29 Jan 1898 p.4g-h
109 WCA CA 1896-1914 p.200 dated 2 Jun 1904
110 In addition to the Boyd family's generosity, there was a subscription fund, the account for which survives in WCA. For further information on the work of the Hele family, and a passing reference to the organ in Winchester, see VERNE, D. Batigan: A Visit to the West Country in *The Organ*, Vol. VII (1927-1928), p.231
111 The gift of the Hon. Mrs Henry Bligh in memory of her husband.
112 WCA CA 1896-1914, p.244 f dated 24 Apr 1906 and p.296 dated 31 Mar 1908
113 WCA Org Misc, Report of Harrison & Harrison dated 4 May 1922
114 *ibid.*
115 WCA CA 1929-1939 Feb to Jun 1931 *passim*
116 See RANNIE *op. cit.* p.203 ff
117 RHODES, Harold: The Winchester Cathedral Organ in *The Musical Times*, August 1938, p.617
118 RANNIE *op. cit.* p.203
119 WCA Accounts Ledger A/c G1 - Cathedral Repairs: Three payments — 15 Feb 1937 £1,500; 29 Jan 1938 £1,500; 16 Dec 1938 £1,150
120 RHODES *loc. cit.* and WCR Vol.VII (1938) pp.9-11
121 Letter from A. Thompson-Allen to *The Musical Times*, September 1938, p.697
122 WCA CA 29 Jan 1963 and 25 Feb 1963
123 For further detail on the thinking behind the design of the Nave division, see VENNING, Mark: Nave and Bombarde. Aspects of Organbuilding for Cathedral Congregations in *The Organbuilder*, Vol.VII, May 1989, p.4

Detailed historical information concerning the past Organists of Winchester Cathedral can be found in SHAW, H.Watkins: *The succession of Organists*, London, 1990, p.292. Although published only recently, the majority of the biographical work was carried out in the 1960s, with additional entries to bring the lists of incumbents up to date.

Figure 5: *Plan of the ritual Choir of Winchester Cathedral*

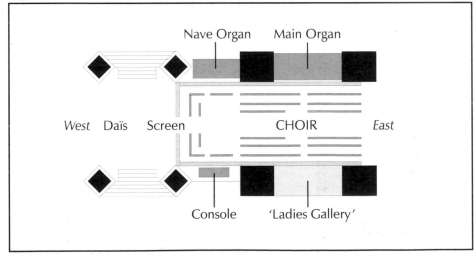

West   Daïs   Screen   CHOIR   East

Nave Organ   Main Organ

Console   'Ladies Gallery'